Are You Highly Favored?

An Ordinary Life with Extraordinary Results!

BY
JOAN STEWART

Copyright © 2016 by Joan Stewart.

All rights reserved.

ISBN 978-1-62806-107-9 (print | paperback)

Library of Congress Control Number - 2016945981

Published by Salt Water Media
29 Broad Street, Suite 104
Berlin, MD 21811
www.saltwatermedia.com

The cover image is used courtesy of unsplash.com via the Creative Commons Zero license with special credit to Emre Gencer. See unsplash.com for more details.

Scripture quotations, unless otherwise noted, are taken from the King James Version of the Bible.

Dedication

A special dedication is given to my husband who encourages me to follow my dreams. Being a mother to our two sons has taken me on an adventure that I could have never imagined. Our four grandkids are the icing on the cake. All of them bring happiness to my heart and smiles to my face. My Mom and Dad and brother were the first to shower me with unconditional love. Each of my fourty-four first cousins have touched my life in their own unique way. The joy they bring to my life is priceless.

About the Author

Joan Stewart is a retired operating room registered nurse and first assistant. After graduating from Sinai School of Nursing in affiliation with Towson State University in Baltimore, Maryland, she made her home in Dover, Delaware.

Along with her husband Jonathan, they also owned and operated a karate school in Harrington and Dover, Delaware for sixteen years.

For thirty years, she has been the First Lady at St. John A.U.M.P. Church in Chester, Pennsylvania, where her husband is the pastor.

They have two sons and four grandchildren.

They reside in Magnolia, Delaware.

Table of Contents

Introduction
- 11 -

CHAPTER ONE: Wonderful Parents
- 13 -

CHAPTER TWO: Here Comes the Groom
- 17 -

CHAPTER THREE: The Boys ... Our Sons
- 27 -

CHAPTER FOUR: Our Time of Challenges
- 33 -

CHAPTER FIVE: Travel Adventures
- 48 -

CHAPTER SIX: Marriage
- 54 -

Introduction

This book is dedicated to all who would read and benefit from the words that are written. God has gotten my attention in various ways about being highly favored as one of his children, so I am indeed inspired by God's prompting to write this book to glorify His divine presence in my life.

I know it was God's urging and not my own pursuit to write again, for I have written three books prior to this over a number of years. None were published. One came somewhat close, but I chose not to labor over it any longer. My desire to write again had long left my list of accomplishments. I came to the realization that I was writing for my own edification and attention. I thought that being a published writer would garner the affirmation that I desired. I thought it would give me an impressive résumé with my family, friends, and associates. I also learned that if God's not in it, why bother. As you see, writing again was nowhere on my agenda.

What does it mean to be highly favored? What qualifies a person to be highly favored? If we get our cues from the present culture, some would think it's the glitter, the glamour, the big mansions, fancy cars, and the endless wardrobe. Or can it be a couple of celebrated events that change the direction of our lives? Can it be a rescue from a life-threatening situation? Or is it a continual series of desires granted that has no other explanation, except the divine intervention of God?

I do invite you in on my ordinary life with extraordinary outcomes and you can answer that question for yourself.

Chapter One:
Wonderful Parents

The first gift that God favored me with was my parents. They were incredible! My dad, who is deceased, was so funny. He kept us in stitches. Everywhere he went, he was the life of the party. He came from a highly social background. His father was a minister and his mother was a music teacher. His father was very gregarious and a love for people was passed down to my dad.

He loved young people and wanted to know all about them and they gravitated to him. My parents had some friends in the neighborhood that would leave their family reunion to come to my parents' house to visit with them. Everyone loved my dad.

Dad had a way of turning practically any situation into a humorous one with his quick wit. I love to laugh, and to me, Dad was the quintessential entertainer. He kept us laughing all the time.

Dad was also a very caring person. My parents were far from well off, but the people in our small community knew that they could come to Mom and Dad and they would do whatever they could to help them.

Once we were on a fishing outing at a local beach. My mom and my brother and his wife were busy fishing and Dad and I took a stroll down the beach. We were talking and he asked me how I was feeling. It wasn't just a polite *"How are you doing?"* with an answer of *"Fine."* and *"Let's continue our conversation."* type of question. He sincerely wanted to know about my health and if I had any problems with my health. I am the nurse in the family and the one concerned about everyone else's health and not really obsessed about my own. When he asked me that question, I was so impressed that he was serious about knowing the state of my physical being. I have never forgotten that conversation although it was many years ago.

When I was in high school and I needed a special belt for the next day in class, my dad took me all the way in town to purchase it. We lived out in the country and town was about twenty miles away. For us who usually went to town to shop only on Saturday, it was a big deal. The next day, I was telling my friends that my dad took me all the way in town the night before to get my belt. When the smartest and the most popular girl in class said that her dad would have never done that for her, there were no words to express how special I felt. That's the kind of dad I had.

I could not have been more favored than with a loving and sweet mom. She showed me through her actions how true Christian love is expressed without saying a word. When I was a young girl, she would take me to my grandparents' house and we would check on them and clean for them just about every day. She didn't have to do that every day because she had other siblings, however she never complained.

One of our neighbors was a widow. My mom would cook for us and include an extra serving to take to her. "Miss Vi," our neighbor, was a short, stout lady who would smile with such appreciation for the meal she was about to enjoy. Mom delighted in helping others.

Friends and family members trusted her. They knew they could talk to her about anything and it would go no further. She would never give advice unless asked. She would always tell me, "I don't get in married folks' business; it's not a smart thing to do." I have always remembered that with our own grown children. Of course if they ask for advice, I am ready to depart any wisdom that I might have.

At one point, one of her widowed friends was letting her know about her interest in a gentleman. Unfortunately, this gentleman was married. My mom simply said, "If you were married, would you want another woman going after your husband?"

Mother was a great encourager. She would tell me,

from time to time, what a wonderful job we were doing in raising our boys. She could never imagine what a positive affect those words of encouragement had on me. To have that affirmation in an arena where there were no textbooks to guide us was huge.

There was always lots of love and laughter in our house. My brother and I didn't know that we weren't rich. We always had plenty to eat and nice clothes (some hand-me-downs). Our parents did an excellent job providing for us. The best thing my parents ever did for me was introduce me to Jesus, the source of my blessings.

I knew as a child that I was loved and cherished. If I could have articulated these words from my crib, I would have expressed my feelings of being highly favored. God gave me the most wonderful parents in the world. I didn't say perfect, but they were very loving and caring ... funny, nurturing, encouraging, helpful, and absolutely marvelous.

My mom is now ninety-two years old. She lives with my brother and still cooks for them and helps around the house. She is happy and content. That makes me happy!

Chapter Two:
Here Comes the Groom

My husband, Bill, (not his real name) and I grew up in neighboring communities. We both attended the same schools, starting in grade school. It wasn't until high school that we started to notice each other. Bill was extremely charming and polite and he seemed intelligent enough! We had a connection in which we were quite comfortable with each other. It was an easy and relaxed and fun relationship. The more time we spent together, the more I fell for his charm and his wit.

At the same time, I was also attracted to another young man that I had a crush on for a long time. Rob (not his real name) was a fun loving party animal. His parents were much older than the normal age of having kids when he was born. I think that they were kind of tired and he was sort of raising himself. He loved to have a good time. He was cute and extremely interesting to me.

Little did I know that God had already picked out

the one I was to marry. After high school, I moved to Baltimore to attend nursing school and college. Bill enlisted in the Air Force and Rob went to a mechanical tech school in Philadelphia.

Bill and I had stopped our relationship after high school because I felt like I was in love with Rob. They were both miles away from me, but Rob and I continued to communicate.

After a while, our relationship began to cool somewhat and we communicated less and less. I think I became too boring for him. I was very busy with school and adjusting to a new lifestyle, therefore my heartache was eased by the attention that my schoolwork demanded.

Many months later, I received a surprisingly sweet letter from Bill. It was a polite letter just inquiring about school and how I was doing. I was so surprised to hear from him. I was also delighted to hear from him. That letter was the beginning of a serious relationship that has lasted over forty-two years.

As a young girl, I dreamed of my perfect wedding day and a marriage that would be full of love and fun. I dreamed of a family with cute little kids all around and big celebrations like the ones my family had. Family is most important to me. In my mind, I had an idea of how my future would look.

When my husband and I were married, pre-marital counseling was not a popular thing to do. There were no hard questions asked about our expectation of marriage or our expectations of each other. No rule book had been formulated about having a successful marriage. All I knew is what I saw and experienced, observing my parents and their relationship. What did we know!

I went into our relationship wide-eyed, full of love and excitement. I was ready for a grand adventure with this gentle, intelligent, and charming man.

Bill and I were married in my little country church in a small community on the Eastern Shore of Maryland. Five days after our wedding, we moved from the East Coast to the West Coast, thanks to the U.S. Air Force.

Our first home consisted of a little cottage with one bedroom, one bath, a kitchen, dining room, and living room. It was situated off the street behind another house and surrounded by a couple of small houses. I didn't know how to cook very much at that time. I would call my mother and ask her how to cook soup and greens and other dishes. She would laugh and explain it to me. When I was growing up, I enjoyed being outdoors a whole lot more than being inside and watching Mom cook. Wow, did I wish I had watched Mom a lot more than I did.

When I look back over our first year of marriage, I realized that it was only God's amazing grace that allowed me to graduate from nursing school, get married a week later, take boards in between, and fly all the way across country to a new state and a new way of life. I had to figure out how to manage a household, manage the budget, and cook, as well as to establish a happy relationship. Needless to say, Rome wasn't built in a day! We enjoyed that time of discovering the couple that we had created, with challenges and all.

From the beginning of our marriage, God gave me the insight of bonding as a couple against any outside influences. It really didn't bother me that we had moved so far away, even though I was very close to my family. It taught us to depend on each other. I didn't want interference from our respective families (not that mine would ever do that). I knew that we needed this time alone to truly get to know each other and to establish our own way of life.

The state of Washington was a beautiful part of the country. The town of Spokane was nestled in a valley with lots of high mountains and big tall pine trees throughout the region. We met some wonderful and friendly people in Spokane. We have some great memories to treasure during our stay there.

I thought I would like moving around as an Air Force wife. I was completely wrong about that one. One move back to the East Coast and I was done with the moving around part. Less than four years after the move, my husband ended his Air Force career! I was extremely happy about that!

Shortly after our move back to the East Coast, my husband returned to school at a junior college. One of the preliminary tests that were required revealed that he wouldn't be very successful with his academics. I knew those results were not accurate, because I was blessed with a very bright and ambitious husband. Bill believed in his abilities, therefore he didn't let those results influence his pursuit of his degree. He ended up graduating with honors and presiding as president of the Honor Society. It served us well to know that we could trust God and believe in our own abilities. We didn't let those negative test results paralyze us into thinking that we were doomed from the start.

Bill went to work as an electrical technician for the DuPont Company. From there, he worked for a laser company. While at work, he would routinely listen to a religious radio station. After listening for about a year, he rededicated his life to Christ. Shortly after that, he felt the Lord calling him into the ministry.

My first question was, "Are you sure the Lord is calling you to do this? Was His voice loud and clear?" I certainly did not see that coming. Our lifestyle would definitely be changing. I wasn't sure if I was up for the calling! I had no idea what life would be like as a pastor's wife.

Bill decided to return to college for his Theology degree. That decision was met with great apprehension. He had to quit his full-time job, use his GI Bill, and find a place to live in Lancaster, Pennsylvania (we lived in Delaware) where his college was located. The worst part was having to manage our house, raise our first son, and work full-time while he was away. He would come home on weekends and school breaks.

Meanwhile, he was also an assistant pastor of his first church — I said he was ambitious! Bill was accepted to college without any problems. He was able to rent a small room off campus. He was also able to find a part-time job there, working for the post office. When I looked back on that time, I could see how God had orchestrated the whole turn of events.

Prayer was a constant in my life. I prayed for Bill's success in school. I prayed for traveling mercies, I prayed for help with managing our home without Bill, and the list just grew each and every day!

While Bill was doing quite well in school, we struggled financially. Our parents helped as much as they could by helping us with groceries whenever they visited. His mother would make his favorite dish of chili. I would add rice and it would stretch for a few days. My parents would bring us chicken from their freezer and whatever else we needed. What a blessing they were!

No one knew when we had gotten three months behind on our mortgage; however, the bank knew! They were so gracious to refinance (we had enough equity to cover the missed mortgages) and sent us back on track with lower monthly payments. Thank God that never happened to us again. That was absolutely devastating to us because we had always paid our bills on time.

By the time Bill finished his bachelor's degree, he was on the staff at the college teaching part-time. He did that for a short time. A full-time position would require us to relocate or for him to come home only on weekends. We were not willing to sacrifice our family time. That position just wasn't worth the sacrifice.

Shortly before graduating, Bill received his assignment as pastor at his first church. It had a small congregation, made up of an elderly couple, their three grandkids, another lady, and a piano player. It was located in a rural area of Golts, Maryland. Chickens roamed in the yard. I remember walking on wooden planks on the ground leading up to the church. There were old hymnals in the pews that were falling apart. The piano player was playing on an antique piano. One of the elderly ladies would always sing her favorite hymn, no matter what the occasion. We still laugh about that.

Our first Sunday was an eye-opener. My husband and I just looked at each other, not knowing what to expect. However, they were genuinely gracious toward us. We fell in love with those precious people. They even gave us a baby shower for our second son.

The next year, we were transferred from Golts, Maryland to a larger church in the inner city of Chester, Pennsylvania. Bill and I were raised in the country, so moving to the inner city was quite different than what we were used to.

Bill was a very effective leader. He made some important changes in the administration of the church. The insight that he had to solve certain problems and his managerial skills surely took me by surprise. They could have only come from God.

The congregation listened, and the church prospered. With any congregation, there will always be some strong personalities. We definitely had our challenges in that category while dispensing the gospel and glorifying the Lord.

The salary for pastors in our conference was far from being enough to raise a family. Bill was blessed to be able to procure a position with the United States Postal Service. That was a happy day for all of us.

The next year, Bill was able to return to college to work on his master's degree part time. Meanwhile, I had been working part-time in the operating room as a first assistant — that's a registered nurse that assists the surgeon when his partners are not available. I loved my job, but I loved my family and church more.

God knew my heart. He knew it was for Him, my husband, our boys, and family. God blessed me to be able to work part-time for the majority of my thirty-six years as a nurse. Working part-time allowed me to be able to help my husband with whatever project he was involved with. It allowed me to be accessible when my parents needed help with doctors' appointments, shopping, and other business. It also afforded me the opportunity to be available when our kids needed me for school meetings and school projects from grade school, through college and beyond.

I literally thanked God every day for allowing me to work part-time all those years. I thanked Him for knowing me and my desires for my family. Even after leaving my career of thirty-six years, I continue to thank God and praise Him for allowing me to work part-time. I am convinced that I was allowed to continue working part-time for so long because I took the time to literally thank God every day! Yes, yes, I was highly favored!

While working part-time, we were still able to live in a new four bedroom house in the country with acreage for outdoor activities, picnics, and family gatherings. We have driven luxury cars that have performed for years.

When I was young, my dad and I would sit on our front step, especially on Sunday afternoons, and watch the cars. I always loved Volvos. I thought they were a class act. I knew they could take the miles, and we needed it for traveling from lower Delaware to Chester, Pennsylvania every weekend, sometimes in between. God blessed us to be able to get a very good deal on a new Volvo demo, after years of seeing them on the highway. I just knew by faith that one day we would own one! I prayed that it would last ten good years, and then fifteen years came and went. Our Volvo was twenty years old when we finally donated it to a veteran's charity.

We searched for another Volvo, but couldn't find anything that we were happy with. On the same lot were Mercedes. We test drove a 320 model with very low mileage, only four years old and still under warranty. We couldn't believe our ears when he quoted the price! I loved it, so we purchased it. We paid cash!

When we came back a couple of days later to pick it up, the salesman said that he had misquoted the price and his boss was not happy! However there was nothing that could be done about it. We said, "Hallelujah!" We checked the blue book price and we paid $13,000 less than we should have!

But that's not the end of the story. We didn't work one hour for that car. We paid for it with part of an inheritance from my mom, after my dad died. As you can see, you don't have to be rich to enjoy the riches of what God has to offer. He is rich enough for all of His children! *"Delight thyself also in the Lord and he shall give thee the desires of thine heart."* That's from Psalm 37:4. Believe it!

CHAPTER THREE:
The Boys ... Our Sons

We were married almost four years when we welcomed our first little baby boy. Brandon (not his real name) was the love of our life and a perfect gift from God. From the moment he was born, I wanted him to belong to the Lord. My husband and I gave our lives to Jesus, so that we could have a victorious life. We wanted to raise our son in a Christian home, like the one I was raised in. We joined our first church as a family and began our Christian journey. When Brandon was born, I was working full-time as a registered nurse in the operating room. At that time, most places of employment only granted new moms six weeks of maternity leave. Where I worked, however, we were given the option of up to six months of leave, without pay. I was able to take almost six months off with Brandon. I couldn't thank God enough for allowing me the extended time to bond with our first born. He was certainly a delightful child.

The end of the leave came way too soon. My heart was broken when I had to leave my baby and return to work. Friends from our church had recommended a very nice lady to watch Brandon. We were extremely happy to have found a highly recommended daycare provider.

Brandon grew to be a very polite child. He was also extremely thoughtful and sensitive. Brandon excelled in his schoolwork, making the honor roll through most of his marking periods. At the age of ten, we were discussing college options — I believe in setting your children up for success at a young age. As he got older, he had his goals and plans mapped out. He was definitely goal-oriented.

When Brandon was ten years old, I began working part-time after the birth of his brother. At the age of twelve, he was awarded the YMCA Youth Volunteer of the Year. He was the type of child that loved to please others.

Brandon was extremely popular and our phone seemed to ring constantly! This was before cell phones were popular. He played basketball in high school and was a take charge type of player. He was often featured in our local newspaper for his accomplishments on the court. He also received awards for his academic achievements. He was accepted to the University of Delaware with academic scholarships. He did well in college. He was also able to find work to help pay for some living expenses.

Brandon received his Master's Degree in Special Education. He was also a contributing writer for a textbook that helps to evaluate the specials needs student. He had job offers waiting for him by the time he graduated. Brandon did all this in five years.

Even though I was working part-time, we were able to pay the unpaid part of his tuition that the scholarships didn't cover!

Brandon graduated without having any student loans! That was a gift his dad and I wanted to give him – a start in life without debt. There was only one way that it was accomplished. It was through our faith in God and believing that all things are possible through Him!

Before our second child was born, I wondered if it was possible to love another child as much as we loved our first born. I wondered if there was enough love in me to share with two kids.

When they put Jared (not his real name) in my arms, I knew right away that he was another precious gift from God. He expressed his opinions so loudly that the nurses had to put him in a separate place because he was disturbing the other babies. However, when he was with me, he was content and happy. God answered my questions with a resounding, "Yes!" It was possible to love this child as much as I loved our first born.

Jared was a strong-willed child from the beginning.

That can be good in some ways and it can be not so good as well, however, Jared was imaginative and bright. He was also highly affectionate and he loved to give hugs. He enjoyed nothing more than holding onto his mommy.

From a very young age, Jared was a people person. Everyone loved his little charming personality. He was adorable. It was very easy for him to relate to others as he got older. Jared had lots of friends and was involved in lots of activities.

By the time Jared was in high school, he informed me that he had some ADD (Attention Deficit Disorder) going on. He tried to explain to me that it was hard for him to focus and concentrate in class. I figured it was an excuse for his grades, but I observed that in the subjects that he really loved, he was receiving A's. In the less interesting classes, he did minimal work. This was our battle through high school. Yet before high school, he received all kinds of academic awards as well as being inducted to the Junior Honor Society. They even wanted to test his IQ, which I would not allow them to do. What purpose would it serve? I didn't want him to think he was superior to anyone.

There were many nights when Jared was the main subject of my prayer time with God. He did however graduate from high school with a B- average. To this day, I count that as one of God's miracles! Considering on the second day of Jared's senior year, he told me that he was bored and done with high school! I told my husband that it was going to be a very long school year!

Jared was accepted into college as a business major. Thankfully, he received some academic scholarships as well. As stated earlier, Jared is very personable. Consequently, his charming personality landed him in the position of being a spokesperson for the college. He could be heard on the radio promoting his college as well as in the local newspaper. He was also the subject on a big billboard on I-95 in Wilmington, Delaware as an advertisement for the college. We could hardly believe the accomplishments of this kid in such a short time period.

Jared had a very active social life, and as a result, his grades began to slip. At the same time, he started working on an invention that occupied a lot of his time! Between those two interests, Jared ended up with an associate's degree as opposed to a bachelor's degree.

We were not thrilled with Jared's decision to leave college. He only had about another year and a half to completely finish. Nevertheless, he came, he conquered, and he was done! That's our Jared! You gotta love him!

After college, Jared managed a restaurant for a while before his reserve unit was called to Iraq. It was a difficult time for us, having him over there. Yet at the same time, I had a sense of peace about it. We kept him in constant prayer. Our whole church congregation was praying for his safe return. I not only prayed for his safety, but I also prayed that he wouldn't be in combat and experience all the carnage of war. I didn't want him scarred mentally and have his loving personality changed. My reliance on God kept me at ease and confident that he would return to us.

God is so wonderful to answer the prayers of His children. Jared returned home safely without firing his weapon once! He did see the poverty and the struggles that country faced, however, that only made him more appreciative of his life in America.

Jared not only returned unscarred, he returned with a lovely lady he met in training, who later became his wife. Their relationship helped them both to endure their time over in Iraq. We are indeed thankful for our daughter-in-law.

Brandon and his wife (although they are not together now) gave us two grandchildren. Jared and his wife also gave us two grandchildren. We are blessed beyond measure and highly favored with our sons and their families. The fact that they love the Lord makes them not only accomplished, but also wise.

We are so grateful that God protects our family, our children, our grandchildren, and the rest of our family members.

Chapter Four:
Our Time of Challenges

As with any family, there are challenges on top of challenges, however God's word tells us to lean on Him – for His yoke is easy and His burdens are light. We are also to know that He will never leave us or forsake us. Those truths served us remarkably well in our times of trouble.

My husband has the type of personality that when he is interested in something, he dedicates his whole being to that project. That single-mindedness does not let him waiver to the right or to the left. That describes the situation when Bill decided to return to the pursuit of his black belt in Tae Kwon Do.

Bill had taken martial arts many years before as a pastime when he was in the Air Force and stationed in Thailand. At first, it was absolutely neat to see him excited about the possibility of achieving his black belt.

We immersed ourselves in the culture. We enjoyed learning about their customs and we certainly delighted ourselves in the Korean cuisine. It was terrific. Then gradually, it became the dominant interest in Bill's life. Our whole world, it seemed, revolved around martial arts. He was not only taking class, but he started teaching as well. His main focus was doing whatever he had to do to please the Grand Master. Needless to say, many, many hours were spent at the do jang – much to my chagrin.

We engaged in countless conversations about the time and energy spent away from his family. He either couldn't or wouldn't acknowledge the affect that his absence was having on our family.

It was an extremely difficult time for us. I was truly distraught! I ended up saying to the Grand Master, "You are going to be the cause of our divorce!" I immediately regretted those words as soon as I said them. That was totally out of character for me to utter such words. I felt like I was fighting for my life. Of course, Bill was upset with the comment and the Grand Master just looked at me, totally surprised. Needless to say, he didn't know what was going on with my husband and me.

One day, I happened to be talking to the wife of another student who was also pursuing his black belt. We were having a general conversation when she started complaining about the unreasonable amount of time her husband was devoting to the Grand Master and Tae Kwon Do. I felt relief in knowing that it wasn't just me being unhappy with my husband spending so much time at the school. I felt more justified with my feelings of being neglected, however, that did little to resolve the situation.

Our circumstance literally brought me on my face before God – pleading with him about my inability to deal with this problem. I told God how totally unfair this was to me and how I felt completely taken for granted. I was laying it all out before God. When I completed my heartfelt outpouring, God so clearly responded to me in a way that I will never forget. He spoke to my heart as if it were audible. He said, "Who are you talking to – about being treated unfairly and taken for granted? You know what they did to my son on the cross. You know how they treated Him and how He suffered and died for you. Do you think they treated Him unfairly? Do you think He deserved that?"

At that point, my whole attitude changed. He also let me know that this very thing that I was complaining about would one day save my life. I had no idea what that meant at the time, but a few years later, those words would ring true. After taking in everything that was revealed to me in our intimate conversation, I felt so ashamed that I complained so venomously. Believe me, I never whined again about being treated unfairly.

I know what Jesus went through on the cross for me. My degree of discontentment could never compare to his agony.

That day literally changed my whole stand about my husband's unwavering pursuit of his black belt and all that it entails. I stopped complaining so much and I gave it to God and relaxed about the whole situation.

Some of our challenges forced us to take a huge leap of faith. You know how life sometimes throws you a curveball that you never saw coming? That is exactly what happened to us.

Bill had been working for the post office for about thirteen years on the day shift. Then his position changed and with that came a shift change. His shift changed to the night shift. He worked it and he was having a difficult time with it. Trying to stay awake was torture for him. He couldn't sleep very well during the day. He was becoming extremely stressed out. The stress was affecting every aspect of our relationship. He would drive home half asleep. The whole situation was wearing on our whole family.

We discussed whether there was any way he could return to the day shift or possibly return to his previous position. That didn't work out. To no avail, Bill tried everything he could think of to survive the night shift and to continue working for the post office. It was not a good time for any of us.

This went on for about nine or ten months and there seemed to be no end in sight. My prayers about our dilemma were long and intense. Finally I said to

Bill, "Please, please just leave. We'll make it somehow."

Ever since earning his black belt, Bill had talked about opening his own karate school. I would reply, "Sure, honey, someday." However, as the post office crisis grew, the more attractive the karate school began to look.

We had long agonizing discussions about what to do. I knew we couldn't continue to live like we were living under the strenuous circumstances. I said, "Honey, please go ahead and open your school. I don't care if we don't make a penny! We can't go on like this!"

It was then that I realized what God had said to me six years previous, about how Bill's interest in karate would one day save our lives. Never underestimate God's word spoken to your heart. His word never returns void. I learned those principles during our turbulent times.

We took a huge leap of faith to make this dramatic change in our lives. We opened our karate school and after the first year, we had to move to a bigger space. Seven years later, we moved to a larger city and doubled our space again. I was in continuous prayer for our school. We had our struggles from time to time, yet almost fifteen years after opening, we are still teaching karate. God is so true to his word! We can trust him in every aspect of our lives.

My personal, huge leap of faith occurred when I had to make a life-changing decision: should I leave my position as an OR nurse after thirty-six years of service?

I loved my job! Being in the OR where everything was up close and personal was so exciting to me. Being an OR nurse meant you had to be organized and knowledgeable and ready to perform in any emergent event. You had to be ready to perform because time was of the essence.

I remember on one occasion, while being on call, our team had to literally run from the cafeteria to the OR to prepare for an emergency case. It was just like you see on TV. It was exhilarating and I loved it! On another occasion, I had to hold my hand over a stab wound that was bleeding profusely while the doctor prepped the patient for surgery.

At another time, while I was waiting for my patient to be brought to the OR, (there was some kind of hold up for a few minutes) a real emergency case was wisped by me and put across the hall. I didn't wait to get official orders from the front desk; I just reacted and hurriedly went across the hall and scrubbed in for the case! It was a terrific feeling to have helped facilitate in the saving of someone's life without having a committee meeting first!

The examples are endless! The doctors and nurses and technicians, for the most part, all worked well together. I enjoyed the comradery and the special bond that the OR staff developed. It especially helped that I worked only three days a week, which I continue to thank God for! I wasn't involved in all the politics and some of the personality issues and so forth that can plague a tight knit group.

Yet, after many years of working in the OR and taking call and getting up in the middle of the night and putting up with all the non-patient specific issues, I was ready to leave. I began praying about leaving long before I was able to leave. I was so ready to go that I prayed, "God, please. I am asking for a miracle so that I can leave today!" I was getting tired and I was ready to move on. A couple of my close friends had left and the atmosphere just wasn't the same as it had been. I prayed that God would give me the patience and stamina until my time came to leave.

Meanwhile, a new neurosurgeon came on staff. I was assigned to be in charge of the neuro department. That was a godsend, because it breathed new life into me. It was new and innovative and exciting. God wasn't ready for me to leave yet. I learned so much, and with the neuro staff, we helped a tremendous amount of patients.

That surgeon retired and others took his place. I also worked in the various other specialties and I enjoyed that as well. Nevertheless, thirty-six years of taking call was more than enough for me.

Still, after all the years in the OR, the decision to finally leave was agonizing. I knew that I had to adjust to a change in income. I also had to let my license expire. That really scared me because if the change of jobs didn't work out, I would not have a nursing career to return to. Some of my other friends had retired early, but they continued to keep their license current, just in case. I would also be retiring early - much earlier than the normal age.

Unfortunately, my husband did not completely agree with my plans and desires. He asked if I could make it to forty years and then go. I knew in my heart that there was no way that I would make it to forty years. My heart just wasn't in it. I knew that if anyone wanted something bad enough, then they could adjust to anything. I was willing to adjust to a different lifestyle if necessary. Bill came to realize that I was genuinely sincere in my desire to leave. I took that huge leap of faith and left the OR after thirty-six years of service. I joined my husband full-time at our karate school.

I have to admit that I was still apprehensive about the decision even months later. In spite of that, I trusted God that it was the right decision to make.

There were days when Bill and I would butt heads about specific issues concerning the school. Those were the days when I would question out loud, "What was I thinking?"

Our karate school was not the first business venture that we tried. My husband has always been a great visionary. I have always been by his side, supporting him, encouraging him, and working with him on our various business ventures. Bill for many years had been desirous of owning his own business. While still working at the post office and even before then, he was involved in side businesses. He is always looking ahead and moving forward.

We had a burglar and fire alarm business for a few years. My husband has made and sold patio furniture. We have made customized children's books. We have sold unique gift products along with household products.

One of my favorite businesses that we were involved in was our Debt Freedom business. We taught people how to get out of debt. It was amazing and a huge blessing to be able to witness our clients' reactions when discovering they could be debt free. On one of the Christian radio stations that I listened to, there was a Christian financial expert named Larry Burkett. He would educate his listeners on how to get out and stay out of debt, and save money. I listened so much that I could answer the various questions that the audience would call in about. I convinced Bill to listen in as well. I know he got tired of me always saying, "Larry would say this is how to handle this situation." I loved Larry Burkett!

Listening to Larry's program convinced me of God's plan for His people as far as finances are concerned. I realized that God doesn't want us to be in debt. He wants us to be free of that slavery. We are to be able to freely give to the promotion of His kingdom. Indebtedness puts our main focus on our finances and that's never a good position to be in. We not only used those principles for our own benefit, but we also wanted to help others experience this freedom.

We conducted seminars to teach the principles that would help people get out of debt. People's lives were changed. Their reactions to knowing the possibility of getting out of debt and staying out of debt were priceless! We loved it!

We were able to retire our original thirty year mortgage in sixteen and a half years! Hallelujah! That accomplishment allowed us to take advantage of so many opportunities that we would have otherwise not been able to do.

Being out of debt played a huge part in my husband making the life changing decision of opening up our karate school and leaving the post office. Only God could have orchestrated that game plan.

A few years after we had moved on from that business venture, one of our hosts from one of our seminars related the following story to us.

There was a young lady that had attended one of our seminars. She was so far in debt and saw no way out so she had decided to take her life that night. She was hopeless. She decided that she would attend the seminar with a friend and later that night, she would end her life. She listened intently and took notes. She saw plainly how she could work with the formula and get out of the burden of debt that weighed her down to the point of wanting to end her life. Coming to the seminar had literally saved her life. It gave her hope and a plan to turn her financial life around.

Bill and I were speechless when this story was shared with us. My husband and I looked at each other, not knowing what to say. We were elated that we were used mightily to impact someone's life. God indeed works in mysterious ways, His wonders to perform.

We have learned and realized on this fantastic journey, that we don't have to be making tons of money to be in the position to help others. God puts the circumstances of others on your heart and it is up to us to act on that – prompting or not.

As with most Christians, we genuinely have a heart of compassion for others in need. God has blessed us enough to help those that we can. It is positively more blessed to give than to receive.

God has allowed us to help others with mortgage payments, medicine, medical bills, vacations, electric bills, clothes, college tuition (not our kids), burned out victims, and scholarships to attend our karate school. We have also given cars away (we have also received cars when we were struggling.)

The year that my parents celebrated their fiftieth anniversary, we were celebrating our twenty-fifth anniversary and my brother and his wife were celebrating their twelfth anniversary. To celebrate, we all planned a trip to Hawaii. Bill and I were treating my parents to Hawaii that year. After we invited them for the celebration, we then had to figure out how we were going to pay for it. The cost included five plane tickets (including our youngest son) and two hotel rooms on the beach of Waikiki! I told my husband not to worry. I just knew it would work out somehow.

Wouldn't you know that God provided in a very surprising way! That was the same year that we received over seven thousand dollars back on our income tax refund! Wow! Does God come through or not!

One year when our sons were younger, we were planning our vacation to go to Disney World. Of course the kids were excited and anxiously anticipating the trip. At the time, our babysitter had a ten-year-old son. He listened to our boys' enthusiasm about the trip and all the fun they were going to have. As a typical ten-year-old, he was caught up in all the excitement and he told his mom that he wanted to go. His mom explained to him that he couldn't go at this time, but maybe sometime later they would be able to go to Disney World. Of course, he was crushed.

That night, I asked Bill if he thought it was possible for us to take him with us. We knew that his circumstances would not allow him to take that trip anytime soon. I was so delighted that my husband agreed to take him with us. It was a huge blessing for us to be able to share our vacation with him. Needless to say, he was ecstatic and his mom was truly grateful. We all had a fantastic vacation.

We not only had many challenges in our personal life, but we also had a catastrophic event with our church in Chester, Pennsylvania. We had been at our church for about eight years when we received a dreadful phone call at eleven o'clock at night from one of our congregants: "Our church is on fire and it's burning down!" We were in bed and we bolted upright in disbelief. We were in shock!

When we met with the congregation, we were all trying to console one another because we were all so devastated. We were only able to salvage a few items from the rubble. A few hymnals, a few Bibles, a couple of Bill's robes, and some communion vessels were among some of the items saved. The question we were all contemplating was this: "Where are we going to worship and what are we going to do?"

We met with our bishop and we were able to worship with one of our sister churches about twenty minutes away. We did that for a few Sundays until we were invited to use the Salvation Army Sanctuary a few blocks away from our original church. We were certainly thankful for their generosity.

We eventually found out that the fire was deliberately set; however, the police never found out the persons responsible for the arson. Thank God we had good insurance on our church. We started making plans to rebuild on the same lot. With the estimates that we obtained to rebuild the church, we found that we would have to have a mortgage! The church hadn't had a mortgage for many years! We were not thrilled or prepared to incur such debt. However, we thought we had no choice.

It is absolutely amazing to witness God's miraculous powers when it comes to providing for His children. While we were still planning for the rebuilding of our church, a huge Catholic church went on the market. Our congregation met with our bishop and we looked over the property. He was in agreement that the property looked like a great investment for our congregation and our conference! We were ecstatic! It needed a small amount of cosmetic work inside, but other than that, we were thrilled. The sanctuary was huge and very ornate. It was breathtaking to view the sanctuary for the first time. When the sun was shining through the large, stained glass windows, the whole scene was ethereal. Everyone who enters the church for the first time reacts with the same awe inspiring response. It is unbelievably beautiful. The sanctuary can seat about five hundred people. The downstairs church hall can hold about five hundred people. Our old church held about one hundred people total. We were certainly blessed with the expansion of square footage.

The best part of it all is that our insurance covered the entire asking price! We even had enough money left to get new hymnals, new Bibles, and a few other items that were needed! The first Sunday that we worshiped in our new sanctuary was a hallelujah celebrating time! We could not stop rejoicing about how God had surely provided for us! We have no mortgage. We have a much larger parking area. We have new Bibles and hymnals. We have an incredibly beautiful sanctuary. We have a huge dining and stage area. Most of all, we have witnessed God's marvelous work.

Chapter Five: Travel Adventures

One of my passions in life is to travel. I love to visit new and different places. I love to take in the sights and embrace the local culture. I have always loved to read maps and I taught my boys when they were growing up to study the maps as well. They were encouraged to point out the various places that they would like to visit. I loved that our sons were very much interested in traveling. Every place that we visited and every adventure that we experienced, I loved. I've never had a bad vacation! There have been some unexpected events that have occurred, but that never stopped me from fully enjoying every minute of vacation time.

One of our most memorable vacations was our trip to South Korea. We spent ten days there along with our martial arts group. Part of our trip included a few days in Seoul, one of the largest cities in the world. We visited Mangsang Beach and swam with the Koreans in the Sea of Japan. We explored the largest cave in Asia. That was totally indescribable. We tried all the native dishes from fried seaweed to bibimbap, but stopped at raw crab meat. I couldn't do that. My husband was looking for a McDonald's or Burger King, until he finally found one. Bill isn't as adventurous as I am when it comes to foreign cuisine. He did like the rice and kimchi and bulgogi.

Some adventures turned out to be more than we had bargained for. We were enjoying a nice tranquil canoe trip down the Susquehanna River in Virginia. We were negotiating some low grade rapids without any problems. We were coming upon the last two remaining rapids when all of a sudden our canoe flipped over and we were thrust into the river. We were told that if we flipped over, not to worry because the river wasn't that deep and that we could stand up without any difficulty. Well, guess what ... my feet did not touch the bottom. I definitely panicked for a couple of seconds, even with my life jacket on. I prayed a quick prayer and settled down. I listened to Bill's careful instructions of what to do and we survived! I was so thankful that we only suffered a few scrapes and cuts on our legs from the rocks. I did sustain a small fracture of my index finger, but I could deal with that. In spite of the mishap, we still had a priceless adventure!

On our visit to Hawaii, my husband won a hula contest in Oahu as we all pigged out at a delicious luau.

We also enjoyed a hike up to Diamond Head. It was crazy fun!

On our second visit, we were able to swim with the giant turtles on the beach of Waikiki. That was wild and uncomfortable, so I didn't stay in the water very long. The rest of my family enjoyed it immensely!

The first time we visited Bermuda, my husband was threatened to be arrested because he took a picture of a police officer at work. Apparently that's a no-no over there. He loves to take pictures. Now he knows that cameras are not always welcome everywhere.

On our second cruise there, we delighted in the glass bottom boat ride and watching the feeding frenzy of the hungry fish. Dancing with the natives at one of their outdoor festivals was absolutely delightful!

We were blessed to be able to fly across country to visit California a few times. While on our trip to San Diego, we were fortunate enough to go horseback riding at Camp Pendleton. We also visited Tijuana, Mexico, where I was able to shop and haggle with the merchants with my limited Spanish. I loved it!

While in Los Angeles, we experienced Hollywood Walk of Fame. That was exceptional! We even went window shopping on Rodeo Drive. $400 for a blouse was a little excessive for me, but it was nice to look at. I did buy one small item and I was happy!

On a separate visit to San Francisco, we traveled over the Golden Gate Bridge and touched the great redwood trees. They were absolutely amazing! We loved their sourdough bread that they are famous for! Yum! Yum!

Christmastime in the Bahamas was indeed strange, for an East Coast American. We were listening to "Jingle Bells" and wearing shorts! On a separate trip there, we were able to enjoy snorkeling for the first time on one of their pristine beaches. The beautiful schools of fish that we observed while snorkeling were positively breathtaking!

Canada is a very beautiful country. On one of our vacations to Canada, we took the ferry from Bar Harbor, Maine to the southern most part of Nova Scotia. The drive up the coast to the capital of Halifax was one of the most picturesque drives that I have ever experienced. I fell in love with the region. At one point, we stopped for lunch at one of the parks. There was a hill that I climbed up and looked around and down the hill. It was the perfect replica of a scene from *The Sound of Music* where Julie Andrews dances to "The Hills are Alive with the Sound of Music." Of course, I did a few twirls and pretended I was Julie Andrews. It was fantastic.

On another visit to Canada, we observed one of the wonders of the world at Niagara Falls. It is indeed a wonder to behold!

In the earlier years, while my husband was stationed in the state of Washington, we went camping in the northwestern part of Canada. The town was Nelson, in the providence of British Columbia. Another couple was with us. While the wives stayed at the campsite, our husbands went hiking up the mountain and they viewed a glacier! I was extremely upset that I missed that adventure. I hate to miss anything exciting!

One of God's most beautiful creations is the Grand Canyon. The grandeur of it all is unforgettable! Only God could be responsible for such a phenomenon.

Also while in Arizona, we traveled on the iconic Route 66. The Native Americans fry bread was a delectable sample of the local cuisine.

Furthermore, we were blessed enough to snow ski in the Catskill Mountains and jet ski (for the first time last year) in Nags Head, North Carolina. We were also invited to dance with the Native Americans in the Smokey Mountains.

On our cross-country trip, from the west coast to the east coast, my husband feared for my life when I got too close to the buffalo in Yellowstone National Park. He still reminds me of that crazy maneuver. While there, we also watched as the amazing geysers erupted. What an incredible sight that was!

Whale watching off the coast of Maine was amazing! The whale was so close to the boat that we could see the barnacles on him.

Another indescribable experience was the viewing of the magnificent Mount Rushmore. The talent that it took to create such a monument is totally unbelievable.

These are some of the great adventures that God has allowed us to experience. Every adventure that we experienced, I loved!

As written in the Psalms – *if you put Him first, He will give you the desires of your heart.* The amazing part about our adventures is that we were able to do all this while I worked part-time for the majority of my career. That proves to me that you don't have to be wealthy to enjoy the riches that God has to offer.

Chapter Six: Marriage

Longevity in marriage is unfortunately becoming more and more rare these days. I have been asked how we have managed to stay married for so long. I have even received the comment from a young gentleman that he doubted that he could stay in a marriage for forty or more years.

I have encountered many self-help books on my journey with similar topics such as: ten easy steps to a healthy marriage, three ways to secure a perfect relationship, and five lessons for you and your mate to see eye to eye, for example.

A lot of these books can be very helpful. However, the more I thought about this, the more God revealed that there is only one step and one word for a healthy and satisfied marriage! That step and that word is obedience.

Obedience to God's word – that's all we need!

Obedience is the answer for a marriage to survive and thrive!

When a person is obedient to God's word, they will respect their spouse and they will forgive their spouse. They will also be patient and kindhearted to each other.

We are commanded to love one another as God has loved us. This is the second greatest commandment of all. It's not an option for us! God expects His children to keep His commandments. Jesus speaks to us in John 14:15: *"If you love me keep my commandments."*

Psalm 34 (one of my favorite Psalms) tells us *"the eyes of the Lord are upon the righteous and his ears are open unto their cries."*

Oh, believe me, I sometimes have difficulty keeping his commandments. We have had our issues, like every married couple. When you are in the middle of a heated debate, it is certainly not easy keeping your cool and being tenderhearted. When you feel that you've been taken for granted or taken advantage of, it's so easy to be vengeful and angry. After many years of practice, I've learned not to make matters worse. It's detrimental to become mean-spirited and to escalate. God tells us we are not to sin in our anger. That's a real challenge that we must have victory over, in order to be successful in our relationships.

I have a habit of kissing my husband goodnight whenever I retire to bed before he does. On this one occasion, we had a huge disagreement and I was very upset and angry. I went straight upstairs to bed and I was still fuming. I said my prayers and jumped into bed. Then a conversation with God ensued and God reminded me that I didn't kiss Bill goodnight. I let God know that I didn't even want to look at him right now, let alone kiss him. I was extremely upset, but God convinced me of my shortcomings. I was in tears because I wanted to refuse to go downstairs to kiss Bill goodnight. That was very, very difficult for me. However, I was obedient and in the end, I was glad I did what I was commanded to do. The tension between us definitely dissipated and I went to bed in peace.

God has blessed us with good health and He has enabled us to do what we enjoy. Of course we have our aches and pains from time to time. That comes with maturing, but it doesn't stop us from enjoying what God has allowed us to experience. Favoritism – what a wonderful state to be in!

I pray that you have appreciated a glimpse into the life of an ordinary person who is highly favored of God.

Are you highly favored? Write down your blessings and keep a journal. Tell your family, friends, and associates and glorify His name.

As I am bringing this manuscript to a close, I just experienced an epiphany. My desire to be a published writer began over twenty-five years ago. This certainly bears witness to another truth about God. We need to wait on Him, for He works on His schedule and not ours. We just need to keep the faith and know that He hears us, without question.

Highly favoritism isn't limited to the rich and famous, the brilliant and talented, nor the gorgeous and sophisticated. Favoritism is available to you and to anyone who has a heart for God and desires to follow His instructions. He instructs us to repent of our sins and accept his son Jesus as our savior and then our life will be purposeful!

See you in Paris!

www.ingramcontent.com/pod-product-compliance
Lightning Source LLC
Chambersburg PA
CBHW031429040426
42444CB00006B/757